BITTERSWEET SEVENTEEN

Bittersweet Seventeen

Written by

ANNA JEAN

PALMETTO

PUBLISHING

Charleston, SC

www.PalmettoPublishing.com

Hardcover ISBN: 979-8-8229-4186-1
Paperback ISBN: 979-8-8229-4187-8
eBook ISBN: 979-8-8229-4188-5

To a younger me..
I will always mourn your deep love for the little things. I have tried to carry it on into my newfound adolescence, but I can't seem to do it the same way you did. We made it, it's time to show the world what we've got!
and to my friends and family..
I love you, you made these years worth living through. I could not be anymore thankful.

Foreword

As a writer, I tend to write about things I know. I started writing at the age of barely fifteen, but as I have gathered my years, I feel that seventeen was the hardest. At seventeen, I thought I knew it all. As it turns out, at seventeen you do not know everything. You hardly know anything, though it feels like you have the whole world figured out. I'm not much older now, but I feel as though I am. I know that in another four years, I will feel like nineteen was an age where I was just as clueless as I was at seventeen. Now that I know I will continue to experience this for the rest of my life, I'm prepared for that feeling to come about.

The teenage years are so rough, and this book contains fragments of my thoughts as I experienced them. I have learned that I definitely do not have the world figured out, and I have also learned that you should always do what you feel is right. I feel like putting my younger self's poetry out into the world is right. Somewhere in here, you may read something and make absolutely no sense of it, but that was probably what was going through my mind at the time. Sometimes my own brain didn't even make any sense to me, but that happens to everyone, I was never worried about it. With that I must say, no, the poems about being angry may not be the best, but that is because an exhausted sixteen year old was jotting these lines down on the back of her unfinished homework. The poems about being in love may be corny, but that is because a sixteen year old is writing about a feeling she is feeling for the first time, and she is grinning ear to ear while doing so. I will never claim to be extraordinary or anything of the sort, but I will always claim to be genuine. No feeling is too small, and no thought is too grand. I just hope there is someone in the world who can read something of mine and relate to it, and know that they are/were not alone. It is important that we let eachother feel seen and heard. We are all experiencing life for the first time together. From the ages barely fifteen until nineteen, here is my collection of teenage angst. I hope it finds you well.

It takes an army to be
a prolific writer.
It takes deadly weapons that we know as
words and thought
and love.
It takes one poem,
one book,
one writer.
It takes the gift of one person
to open a world of beauty
to the minds of many,
few,
or just one.

I opened my eyes and recalled the dream that just ended.
You called out for me, in my dream.
One encounter made me smile,
I awakened with a breath of life
I watched my fantasy end.
Your arms slipped away,
Your smile faded.
Your touch got softer,
Your words slurred and your voice trailed off
As if being pulled by something that was just out of
reach.
Though your presence lingered,
Hours passed and i still felt
The tenderness
And melancholy of
The encounter.

She stops dreaming
Her rhythmic breathing
Eradicates and gasps slightly.
The soft skin of her chest has started to twitch in
awakening.
Panic sets in,
As her eyes flutter awake,
She realizes where and who she is.
Her eyelids flutter so delicately
So fast yet gentle
I watch the color of her eyes flash before me as she opens
and closes
In the gently fast motion.
Once they open i am met with the life beside me
The pain of yesterday has subsided
We are left with the mystery of today.

What if I am
All that I will ever be
Right now?

What if my
Introspection of the world
Makes others
Turn their cheeks?

What if my
positivity, childishness,
Creativity, ambition, and
Complex way of wonder
Makes others grimace?

What if I am never enough?
What if my best is never good enough?

But what if it is?
What if I don't drown,
And someone loves me
For my what-ifs?

What if?

I stand in the shower
And let the water burn my skin.
I run until my face is pale
and my body faces exhaustion.

I listen to the things that hurt me,
Words that are thrown at me,
And i absorb
But never speak.

I absorb the discontent that i am told i cause
So that hopefully i will stop hurting those around me
I soften the impact
I let them fall like a feather
I stand here,
Like a sponge
And I absorb this pain.
I live in hope that their minds can wander free
Without me in their way.

I hope one day
Someone comes along
and rings me out
and tells me I don't need to be a sponge anymore.

The air that surrounds my excited body begins to become uneasy.
The trees are dancing slowly, almost eerily,
Swaying at a soft, yet violent rate in the stormy winds.
The atmosphere becomes moist, damp with the oncoming rain.
The air that infiltrates my lungs becomes humid, almost suffocating.
The world becomes silent. The birds are quiet and the wind ceases in my ears.
Then the rain falls, slowly at first.
The wind picks up and the clouds start to sob intensely, heaving themselves breathless.
I can feel the cold droplets of rain on my warm skin.
I can feel the breeze raking through my hair, squeezing through the stitches of my shirt.
I can smell the wonderful scent of the ozone layer, oozing out of the universe.
Because of the rain, my heart is happy,
And my soul is put at ease.

Winter is such a vulnerable time for nature.
The trees strip themselves of their beauty and show their
true structure.
The bushes and shrubs become naked and stay still on
display,
Allowing one to stare, ponder, and observe them.
The wind becomes brisk and the grass and weeds turn a
cold shoulder.
The flowers break down and wilt. The animals have a dire
need for warmth, so they leave quickly with no goodbyes.
Nature becomes numb, only clinging onto hopes that
they will survive.
Just shivering and moving slowly,
Exposed and breaking but surviving, they are vulnerable.

Pity Of War
A poem written during observation
of the painting by Max Ginsburg.

As I lay,
Physical embodiment of my heart in my arms,
I feel all of the warmth, the love that was once there
Alive and breathing
The smiles that were given to me, all of the laughing and
crying we shared.
I felt it all leave.
Surging through my veins,
Pouring out of my eyes,
Screeching through my body,
Loud screams laced with pain.
Many times, my heart seemed to stop and I gasped.
I cried and I cried,
I was alone with empty love and I cried.
As fast as the air entered my lungs,
It left just as he did, and I cried.
Harder, faster, stronger,
Even without consciousness, I cried.

It is felt when you stand up
A chill, cold feeling-
The top of my head is off
When one bell rings,
The touch of a hand is true..
A shattering wave of pure guilt,
Is sure to leave you blue.
I, too, am wild
One seems eager to let go.
Dancing about with rain and fire,
Wind is juggling with every throw.
Erupting like a wave,
Crashing like a plane,
Tears of diamond pierce my skin.
Every heart remains broken
Until not-

I haven't the least bit interested in being steady.
It is with deep indulgence and fascination
That i find myself satisfied, and it is not without
challenge and failure
That I find myself successful.

Fingers, the ones that touch-
With the reverse touch of midas,
And incandescent hatred.
The fingers that ruin, taint, and beat.
The battered limbs that climb into the depths of
destruction
until the thought soaks in her brain, floats in her
memory
Stays like the sun, burning like fire.
My fingers, the ones that touch,
The pressure too strong, they prod too much
My fingers will become bees
In search of a flower.
They didn't realize what they had was enough,
They destroyed and took
From the weak and tired.
The things that weren't there
They should not hold
Something they do not perceive
My fingers spread like wildfire.

Oh the sheets that come undone in the night
Creeping down, wrapping my peaceful body within,
But I wake, wake from a restless slumber.
Unable to remember a moments easy peace
Perhaps there wasn't one.
When I am suddenly unable to fix the sheets that come
undone in the night,
Call for a solitary intervention.

I am not tired.
Though I have taken a restless path,
Into a restless goodnight,
Working through a violent storm,
Walking among a thousand wars,
I am not tired.

She keeps it in the bag until she is ready to reveal.
As if night could just slip away, becoming a barrier of time,
When it begins to spill,
All of her truth unfolds
Nonetheless,
They are welcome.

To be alive is to know of the most grueling chore,
but to finish the chore is to know of the greatest joy.
Being alive is knowing a ferocious fire that spreads into thee,
Until a genuine soul is brave enough to put it out.
A bare truth is living through the years speaking only of heart,
and a kindness so pure, only the wisest will endure your
presence.

Call upon a winter mild
And sweets so soon to be.
Laying upon the flowers so wild
Will surely set me free.

Cease your looming thoughts to none
and crave the touch of thee.
Counting down the days till one
And grow with the evergreen.

Although your lasting days grow thin
and along goes happiness,
the youthful girl who gifts a grin
returned and brough pure bliss.

Standing in solitude
Coarse, brown sand scraping my uprooted limbs,
A harsh beam of light glistens upon my faded and dry
green leaves.
A gust of wind knocks my branches around, and
suddenly I can't breathe.
As I grapple with the world to survive, a man walks by.
His head is held high,
His body is moving easily with grace.
I silently beg for him to stop,
To gift me companionship
To grant me the transience of peace I once had.
I plead for a breath of air
For a touch of life
I watch as the man leaves footprints in the dirt
And his nurtured body gets smaller and smaller
Until it fades to nothing.

For years, I have seen the life of others taken and used
By the men who walked by.
My leaves are an offering of peace that these creatures
take for granted.
I stand there,
The only one left, and i beg for the breath of air that was
taken from me,
I long for the warmth of my fellow trees
And I cry out for the kind touch of others.
But the man walks by,
I beg

I plead
His body fades into nothing.

As im nearing the end
My brittle body doesn't feel as tall
My leaves are a near gray color
And my roots have been scraped until bare.
A woman walks by
Her feet tread lightly against the rough, dry ground.
Her hair blows wistfully in the harsh wind
Stopping in front of my weak, fragile body
I feel a sudden rush of life
A breath of fresh air
Small delicate hands placed upon my
Yearning, decaying body.
I no longer beg, nor plead
She is not fading into nothing,
She is giving,
She is caring,
She is living
And I am finally breathing.

It is with great pride that I tell you,
all of my vital organs have turned to dust.
It is the kind that you wipe off of the bookshelf, or the
windowsill.
The dust that holds smiling faces written by tiny fingers,
I'm a bother to you, aren't I?
I float as you eagerly wipe me away,
However hard you try, I will always collect in the sacred
parts of you.
Books that hold stories of thousands,
Tables made ny the hands of man,
Cabinets that you grab your coffee from every morning.
The corner of your mirror- oh how beautiful you are.
It is with great pride that I tell you I have turned to dust,
because I am every particle of the world, yet nothing at all.

If blue could be happiness
My frail, fragile body
my-ever so delicate- mind
Would be lathered in the richest shade
In the heat of the summer,
my pain shall subside,
and fall into the pits of the ripest fruits.
Joy will paint the sky,
and mend the seas-

It's nothing you've ever hated,
yet something you've always feared,
One day after another,
Then one day we disappeared.

So she left- the girl in white-
Along with her yellow hat
The girl so happy who left me to die
And have a meeting with death.
"Hello sir" he welcomed me in and took my coat and scarf.
He asked me what brings us to meet again,
"The girl left me to rot."

I know a feeling i've only felt on weekends
Honey on my lips
Hands on my every bend.
I knew three words
That lost all meaning
And i knew a girl
Who insisted on leaving.

I cannot take a breath in
Knowing that you are somewhere in this world.
You are somewhere forgetting I exist.
I cannot take a breath
Without you knowing me
Loving me
Perceiving me
I just can't seem to breathe without you.

Dare to disappoint
Love to linger in a looming twist of despair
Guilt is a tragic thing
Pity is deceiving in the least.

More of what came to be a nightmare
Formed the shape of a beast.
The beast from the woods,
Not to fret, for the beast cannot harm you, it only causes
fear.
Though knowing of its existence will eat you alive,
so you are not to feel anything but fear.
Wanting to feel nothing
Is to wish life away.

There is a silence-
I found it in the dead of night
A breeze that flows calmly,
Giggling with the evenings guests
A silence that is found in my own company.
The stars gather to watch the moon,
The grass and the water greet each other.

When peace is disrupted
And you are questioning your own sanity
There is always a sense of light
In more ways than one.
One, two, or a few
A gracious energy
Touching you
Igniting your soul
At once.
Some search high and low
Here and beyond
But it is between us
and them, the light
It is within your light
You will find peace again.

You're going to have to buy
Goat milk soap, the organic one,
From that stand at the market. Your favorite one.
You're going to have to use it
To rid yourself of the clandestine rendezvous
the chemically scented
Store bought soap could not rid your filthy hands of.

Intuition is a powerful thing
Mine is telling me I am a flame.
It is surging through my body,
Like sludge in my veins.
Wrapping around my intestines,
Infiltrating my mind,
Telling me to ignite.
Where it sits in my mind,
A dark, damp place.
A prison of passion I have never been able to escape.
I am a flame,
I tend to ruin things i touch,
Things I feel.
They disappear like my sense of self.
I cannot hold steady hearts on my own, they will rot.
They will burn.
Seeing red is no longer a saying, no longer a myth,
It is me.
You will see me as I, totally unaware, ruin everything
around me.
Nevertheless, feeling guilty straight after,
I'm the killer, I am the fire.
As my soul emerges with another,
They will feel a piece of me spreading into theirs.
Warm and comforting as it may seem, it will
undoubtedly turn to disaster.
They become what I cannot control,
I am left to tame the flame within me,
Within you,
Within anything my embers have touched.

I am fire, a short flame
Leaving a charred path of my existence
Scorching everyone I've ever known
Until they are left with the scars of knowing me, forever.

Observations
Peering over broad shoulders
A glimpse of freckles glazed upon a soft face.
White cloth resting over bronze skin
Smoother than a summer breeze
Glimmering strands of gold hair resting
Upon a thoughtful head
Intuitive blue eyes sharp enough to hurt
But warm like a lullaby.

For lack of better words,
I am a hawke.
Look at the wings I spread.
Feel the gust of wind beneath my head.
I have no intention of wandering,
Though sometimes I do.
I'll always come back again.
I'll never leave home,
and I'll never leave you.

Sterilize the corners
You will not cut until they are clean.
A feeling you've never felt,
A sturdy surface beneath your hands
A ground beneath your feet.
Awaken from your drowning dream,
To see yourself in the mirror
And despise what you've seen
A scar on your cheek that reopens when you smile.
Happiness now a luxury
A life you'll never have,
Always just a wish away
Just hoping someone hears you and listens when you pray.

My favorite flower
grows in the meadow
beyond fields of green,
and there the wind will take you
to see the frolicking bees.

Disperse in an orderly manner,
Cautious when returning the touch of thee
For when they do,
the flowers that bloom
will return annually.

If I could throw the lifeline,
I'd throw it farther than before.
When I raise my voice my dear,
it's love I'm shouting for.
I never mean the words I say,
somehow my face molds to the tone,
but your love for me keeps growing while I scream
through slammed doors.

The bottom of my heart is sick
every muscle is worn down.
I hardly speak a word to you
but I'll always be around.
I hope one day you look for me
and forgive me once I'm found,
If I'm not one hundred
and six feet underground.

I don't believe in miracles,
but you're speaking to me now.
A jumbled mess of nonsense,
I ignore your sweetest sounds.
Thank you and I love you are all you know when I'm
around,
but I mash you up and pour you down,
I hope you wish I'd go to hell.

I think I'm being selfless
when I tie your heart in knots
I tell myself I've saved you from the bullies

and the imaginary rocks.
You're stronger than you know,
Oh how I admire you so, Jo.
I'd give you anything you'd ever need and more if I could,
but for now I'll tell you I love you more than you know.

If you'd come by,
To my home,
where i keep my nicest gown
and my softest sheets
and you told me you love me,
I'd have to suck in my deepest breath.
Id have to tie up my hair,
and pace around the room.
Then I'd finally come out and say
"And I love you"

I like to walk places.
I like to stare at my feet and control the pace at which I
am moving.
I like the sound of the leaves in the trees,
and the wind rushing against my ears.
If i am out early enough,
I like to hear the songs of the mourning doves.
I hope when I die,
The mourning doves sing a song just for me.
I hope whoever hears it
does not find it maddening.

There are few times I have felt the ocean.
When you kissed me
And your warm tears entered my mouth.
The push and pull of your body
As we danced to the rhythm of our own beating hearts.
The crash of your fingertips on my cheeks
when you traced my smile as I laughed.
So it happens, every time i have seen the ocean,
I have felt you.

Standing with you in my living room,
listening to oldies and the sounds of summer 2019.
I can't dance so you let me step on your feet,
I've got no words to speak.
I thank you for the gesture, then get up and leave.
We put a spin on walking to the gas station,
If I get there first I get to play the victim.
Just Pretend we're on a mission,
and hope one of us doesn't turn up missing.
I know i'm shying away again not speaking loud and clear,
I'm just thinking.
I'm never far away,
Ill attest to you,
I'll see it through.
No more lying through my teeth.

The sunlight spills into my room and pours across the floor,
and in the hue of gold and greed it spreads its way to the door.
The winds move in and the tides roll out and the clocks
dials have met,
I will sit like a bird on a power line and wait for the sun
to rest.

The flowers blossom, the leaves fall, the sky will turn to gray,
the sun will be merciless, but come winter she shies away.
The mourning doves will sing their songs and bees flee
from their hives,
the second I hear the doves sing, I will beg for the sun to
shine.

When the moment allows for it, the sun begins to dance,
anywhere the light can pour, spring gives the sun another
chance.
Flowers bloom, the fawns are born, the rain splatters
across the pavement,
I sat on my porch and watched the sun rush in as quickly
as she went.

Please let me watch the sun plaster colors across the sky,
I'll think of you before the blacks and blues take the sun
before my eyes.
The moon opens her eyes and i'll close mine once more,
and when I wake I'm sure I'll see the sun poured out on
the floor.

I once met a girl who worked for her dad on the
weekends.
Who never complained about any situation.
With her worn and tired eyes,
she always took me by surprise,
when she would stay up late with me every evening.
All of her days faded into one when she got busy.
The thought of leaving left her dizzy.
So she just packed her bags and left,
left her heart on the front steps,
and gave her drum set to her little sister.
Her mama would call her on the pink rotary phone
to ask her baby when she is coming home.
To see the twinkle in her eyes,
and how time has gone by,
and whether or not she's still the big eyed girl that she
misses seeing.

I'm breaking my legs
running across the hard ground
as your pickup truck
fills my mind with sound.
How far is it,
to your side of town?
I'll pick up the pace,
I just want you around.
I don't believe in time.
I tend to like it better,
so when I think of when I die,
I can't mark it on the calendar.
You like the way I walk,
I like to tie your shoes.
I love you but something I've learned,
rubber bands don't snap as
quickly as you change your mood.

Misery is a shame
Too late to call, too early to blame.
She is torn for your show
she'll watch as her life goes,
She thinks too much about it.
Moms at the bar, says "forgot about me"
Turn it all off,
dread kills for a bit.
Falls asleep in the backseat,
reap around the corner
Too tired to beg for more.
She's never where she needs to be
but she's survived long enough for me.

He'll keep her around for years
If she remembers, she'll wake up in tears.
Mistakes are made, you learn and you live,
Forget who you are, take it out on your kid,
Call up your brother, forget that he's down,
Mislead your daughter, she's safe and she's sound.
She's stuck on the phone, life goes by in a haze
If she can't find another, she's counting her days
Dread waking every morning
Too tired to beg for more,
She's never where she wants to be,
but she survived enough for me.

I said a lot of things i'm not proud of,
and the words written in fine print
are all my best intentions.

I can't put my body down,
I'm just too much to carry
I can't stay home for too long
Comfortably scares me.

Focus on these brand new plans.
Build around solidarity
When you see I'm too naive
I wont change because I'm not ready
Wait till you find out what I've done
It's the same as when we left things
I'll never grow to be ideal
I'll probably ruin my marriage

Untie the ropes that bound us all together
And watch me fade out
I'll take myself out and find another
But its not cause I want to
I just feel ashamed
Why won't you say my name
I just find someone to blame
as long as it's not me

For what seems like hours
Im staring out the window
I'm fighting with my friends
About absence and limbo
And I forget about myths
That sound more like a promise
Pour my heart into a song
Remember what you said about it
Sometimes I'm red but I'm blue all the time
It's time I come by but I'm too damn selfish
So I'll stand by.

Oh, how you dulled everything with beauty,
but now i'm thirsty.
Thirsty for something I could never have
with you tugging on my sleeve
and you've got this humor sweet as honey
laughing around me
so i could barely breathe
now here you are on your knees
begging me please
come back, you'll see,
all you ever seem to do is repeat.

I'm giving up for the patrons,
the ones who seem to know me better than best.
I'm holding up peace for the sake of man,
with my self worth wrapped around a finger
but it doesn't even fit.

I could have it worse,
but I could have it so much better.
I could have anything I want
if I was just a little taller
and faster and smarter.
Losing myself to daydreams
I know will never happen
And I will probably never snap to my senses.

A bustling crowd slows you down
on your way to the parking lot.
I met you when the light was dim and you
Told me how hard you fought
To keep it together,
To be alright,
To not be so afraid of the dark.

Feast upon the flowers
Prey upon the masses
and shoot like you have power.
Lie to get you farther
Fancy a new blade
Knowing that you can't be bothered
Hide beside your rage
Swung the ax into the wood
Almost missing the tree
Smirking at the thought of killing
Anything that breathes.
Branches snapping beneath your feet
Not caring how loud you seem to be
and you're starving honey,
can't help but rip it up shreds
Snarling
Keeping your teeth barred to the world
Cannot keep the shirt held round your back
Grinding gears for quicker cash
Never ceasing fire the flame turns
Rose to ash.

For my final words, I will not hold back.
I am pleased to be where I am,
Pleased to be who I have become.
It was not without years of discontent and confusion,
Dull aching and self discovery,
That I have been led here.
The pain of yesterday has truly subsided.
I am faced with yet another day and I get to choose.
I get to choose whether or not to dwell,
To seize the day or to sink.
I get to choose whether or not to be great.
I have found that I will always choose to be great.

Thank you.